Online Dating Advice
From The Match Master

The Essential Handbook
For Approaching Women Online

by Alfonso Ochoa

Published by Volossal Publishing
www.volossal.com

Copyright © 2016
ISBN 978-0-9968826-3-7

Introduction

The world of online dating is a cruel place for horny ass guys. You get taken advantage of by sites that hype up how many chicks they have, when they don't really have that many at all. Some sites, guys are getting ignored by girls that they wouldn't bang when they're drunk. Even the sites that have a good amount of girls, there's only a few guys with 6 packs that are doing most of the banging. My point being, online dating is very competitive and you need to bring your A-game.

This is where this book can help. Most messages will be ignored so you need to open a lot. In this book, you will see simple tactical advice followed by an example of this used in practice. So, every single lesson will be followed with a screen shot of a message sent to an actual girl on a real dating site. You'll notice that very few are followed up with a response from the girl. That doesn't even matter. So don't worry about that. The lessons are still good. Trust me.

Also, you'll see that in each individual message I've changed the voice of my character, point of view, job, name, etc. I did this on purpose and you should too. The reason being is that being who you really are hasn't worked so far so why keep doing it? If you have a problem getting laid, then you need to be who you aren't because being who you are sucks and it doesn't work and nobody likes you. So, what I've done is read the profile of each girl and tailored each message to sound like the douche bag that I think she'd be willing to give it up for. The other reason I did this is to show you that no matter what your situation, you can still contact girls to get laid. So, some of these messages will be well thought out lies and other ones will be examples of what to say if you want to be honest about a weird situation. Plus a bunch of other things. By the end of this book, you'll know what to do.

So, you're probably thinking 'What do I do if I lied to get a date?' Easy. Just keep lying until she finds out who you really are. When she finds out who you really are, preferably after you fall in love, she'll appreciate the effort. Just look at it like this, lying is just the male equivalent to putting on make up. So, when she's ready to reveal her true face, that's when you can reveal your true name, job, etc.

Before we jump into the first lesson, you need to know how to read this book. What I've purposely done is made the advice on the right page and put the screen shot example on the following left page. To see the example for the advice you have to flip the page. I did this so you take a beat to let the advice sink in before you see me use it in practice. Read it a few times and reflect on it before you read the screen shot. This will make the lesson more powerful. Lets get started!

Timing

It's not what you say, it's when you say it. This next message is short, sweet and to the point. I sent this message at a time of day that she would know that I wasn't down for just lunch.

Timing

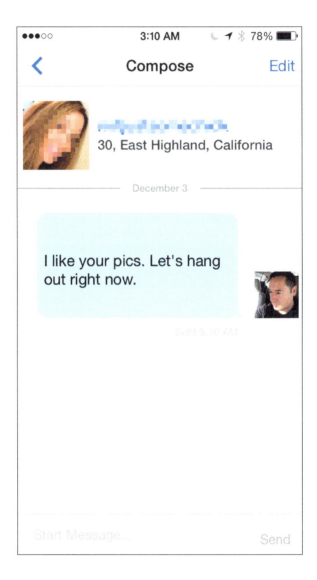

Backing Out

Sometime's when messaging girls, you might come off a little bit creepy to them so always think of a way to back out gracefully.

Backing Out

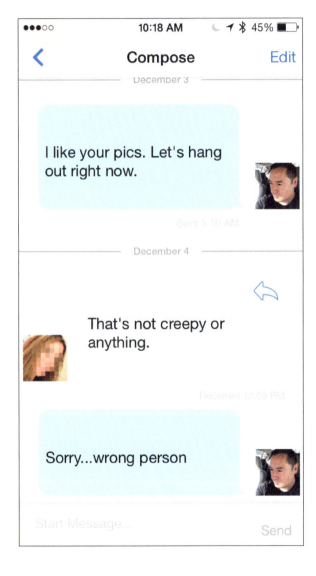

Complimenting

Women love being complimented.
Do it but just don't be too flattering.

Complimenting

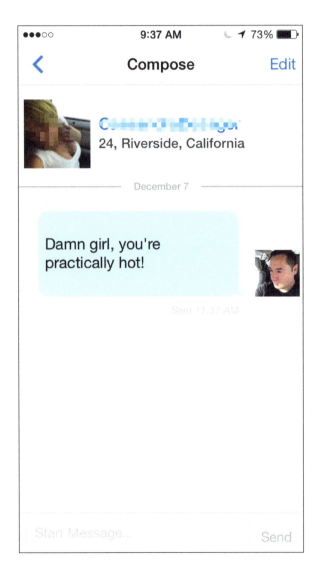

Avoid Holidays

Christmas and Valentines are total rip offs for guys. Wait until after these have passed.

Avoid Holidays

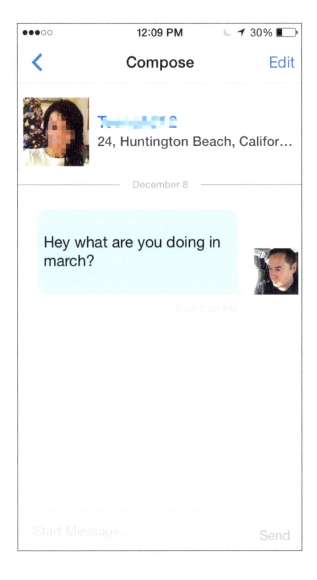

Best Girl

If you come across a profile that stands out from the rest, let her know exactly how she stood out to you.

Best Girl

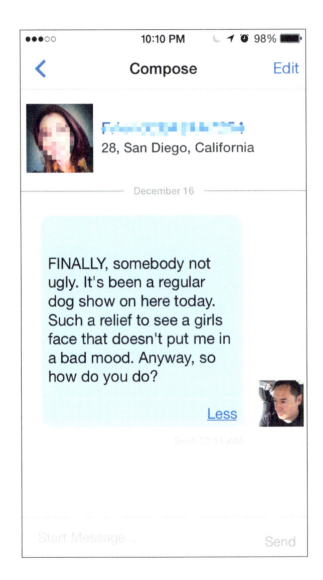

Pulling Strings

Every girl wants to be with a big shot. If you have connections to an upcoming event, flex your power.

Pulling Strings

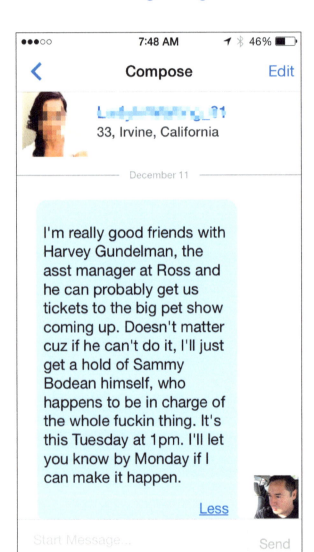

Wolf In Sheeps Clothing

A sneaky but effective tactic is pretending to be gay. It has many advantages. She won't see you as a threat in any way and you can form a strong connection. You're also more tempting to her because she "can't have you". Very effective technique.

Wolf In Sheeps Clothing

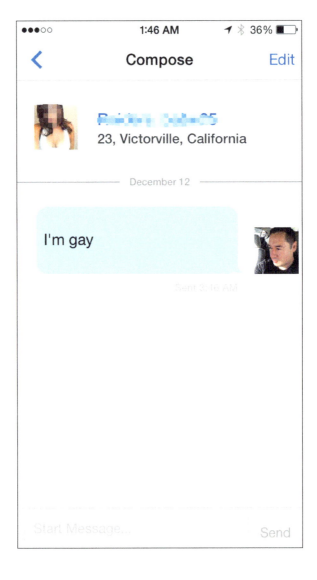

Grillin' and Chillin'

A BBQ is a cheap date and a relaxing atmosphere.

Grillin' and Chillin'

Big Loser

If you had some dramatic weight loss, talk about your accomplishment and how it's affected your life.

Big Loser

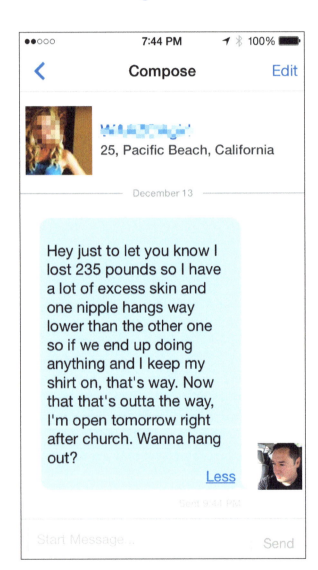

Shopping

After going through her profile and you're not interested, it's ok to contact her for other interests.

Shopping

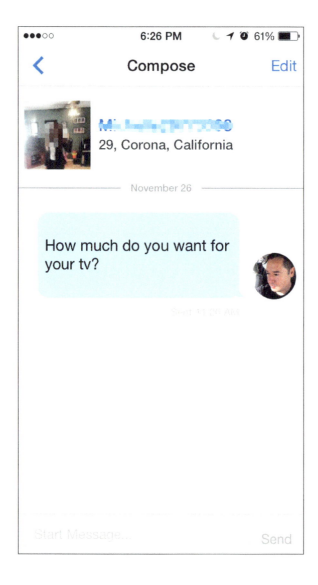

Fill In the Blanks

A lot of times girls will leave important areas of their profile blank. If this information is crucial to you, don't be afraid to request it.

Fill In the Blanks

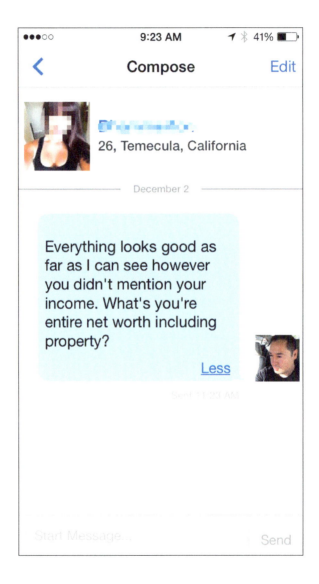

Location Location Location

Try to set up a date where it can be easy to escalate the situation.

Location Location Location

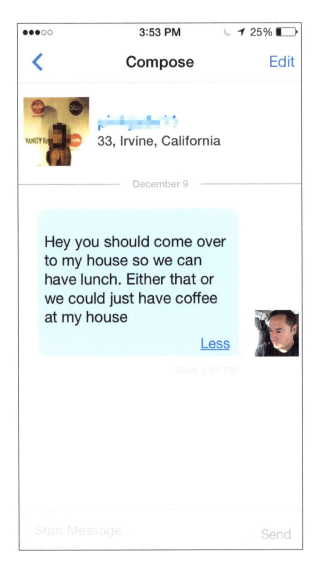

Latin Lover

Women are suckers for the Mexican accent. Faking this accent in your message will lead to way more dates.

Latin Lover

HABLAS ESPANOL?? I only speaking little engish. Right now I learn because I'm liking girls that es white. Si hablas espanol es better and we talk easy. If you no Spanish we still can going to movis and es ok.

Better Times

If life is a little rough for you at the moment,
you might want to hold off before setting up a date.

Better Times

Swaggy

You don't need money or your own place
so long as you approach the girls with swag.

Swaggy

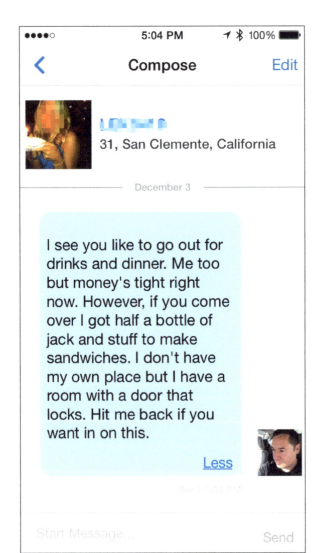

> ●●●●○   5:04 PM   ✈ ✳ 100% ▬▬▶
>
> ‹   **Compose**   Edit
>
> 31, San Clemente, California
>
> ——— December 3 ———
>
> I see you like to go out for drinks and dinner. Me too but money's tight right now. However, if you come over I got half a bottle of jack and stuff to make sandwiches. I don't have my own place but I have a room with a door that locks. Hit me back if you want in on this.
>
> Less
>
> Start Message...   Send

Follow Up

If you really like a girl and you don't receive
a response, be a man
and send a follow up message.

Follow Up

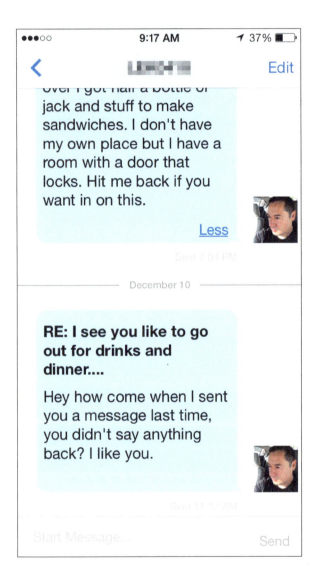

over I got half a bottle of jack and stuff to make sandwiches. I don't have my own place but I have a room with a door that locks. Hit me back if you want in on this.

Less

Sent 7:04 PM

December 10

RE: I see you like to go out for drinks and dinner....

Hey how come when I sent you a message last time, you didn't say anything back? I like you.

Sent 11:17 AM

Start Message...   Send

Swaggy Not Creepy

If a girl tells you that your message was creepy and you know for sure that it wasn't then let her know that she's mistaken.

Swaggy Not Creepy

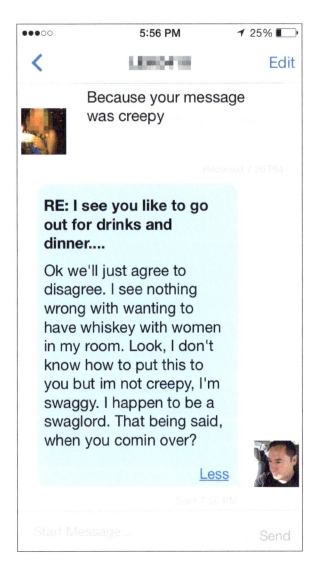

What Happened?

If a girl is divorced, you can get info by having a cool attitude about the whole thing.

What Happened?

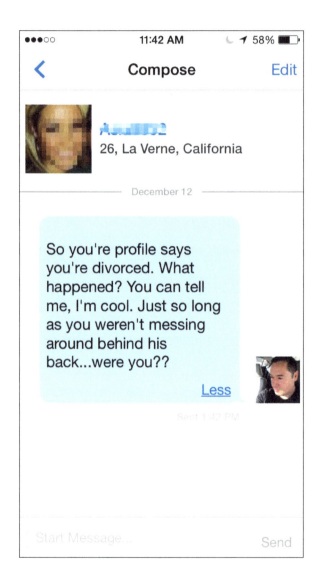

So you're profile says you're divorced. What happened? You can tell me, I'm cool. Just so long as you weren't messing around behind his back...were you??

Planning is Everything

Try to make plans well ahead of time so you can get all of the accommodations you need.

Planning is Everything

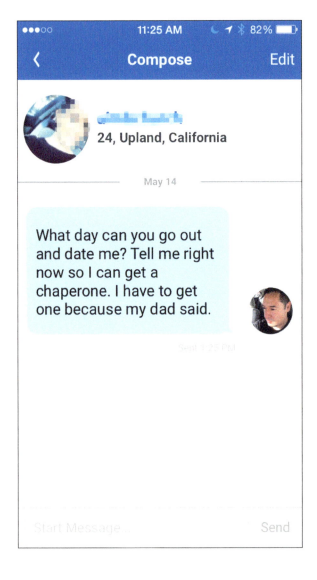

All About Ass

I'm an ass man. If you are too, go ahead and ask for measurements and see if they are to your liking.

All About Ass

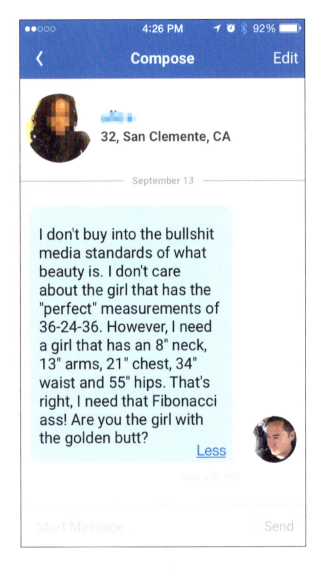

4:26 PM · 92%

Compose

Edit

32, San Clemente, CA

September 13

I don't buy into the bullshit media standards of what beauty is. I don't care about the girl that has the "perfect" measurements of 36-24-36. However, I need a girl that has an 8" neck, 13" arms, 21" chest, 34" waist and 55" hips. That's right, I need that Fibonacci ass! Are you the girl with the golden butt?

Less

Start Message   Send

Name Drop

Nothing will drop her underwear faster than you dropping a celebs name. Even if you don't know anybody famous, just lie.

Name Drop

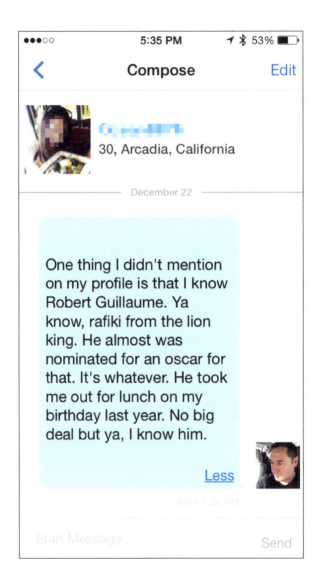

5:35 PM ✈ ✱ 53% ▪▭

‹ **Compose** **Edit**

30, Arcadia, California

—— December 22 ——

One thing I didn't mention on my profile is that I know Robert Guillaume. Ya know, rafiki from the lion king. He almost was nominated for an oscar for that. It's whatever. He took me out for lunch on my birthday last year. No big deal but ya, I know him.

Less

Start Message... Send

Please and Thank You

Women appreciate when you use these words.

Please and Thank You

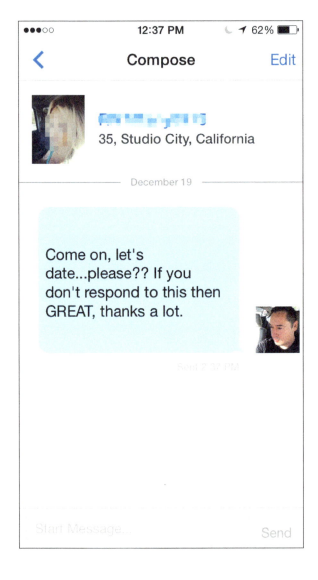

Respect
Talk about the respect you think
you deserve before you set up a date.

Respect

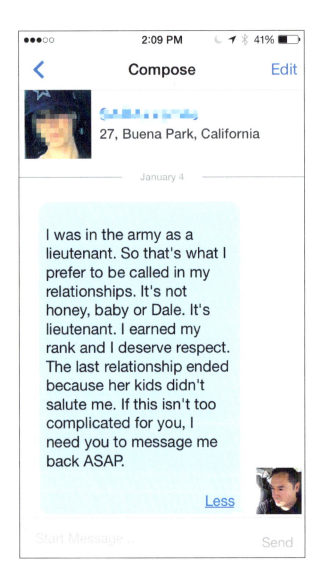

Slang

If you want to hook up with young chicks, use slang.

Slang

Emojis

If you really want to step up your game with young chicks, use emojis.

Emojis

Better Than Money

Just because you don't have money doesn't make you less valuable. Talk about the things you have going for you.

Better Than Money

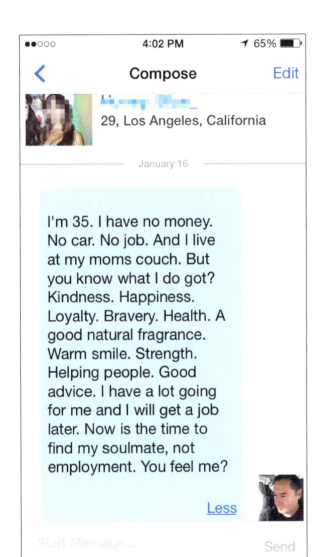

I'm 35. I have no money. No car. No job. And I live at my moms couch. But you know what I do got? Kindness. Happiness. Loyalty. Bravery. Health. A good natural fragrance. Warm smile. Strength. Helping people. Good advice. I have a lot going for me and I will get a job later. Now is the time to find my soulmate, not employment. You feel me?

Be Funny

Women LOVE a man with a sense of humor.
Show her that you have a good one.

Be Funny

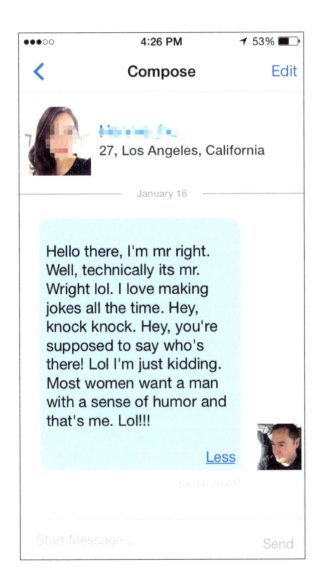

●●●○○   4:26 PM   ✈ 53% ■▬

<   Compose   Edit

27, Los Angeles, California

January 16

Hello there, I'm mr right. Well, technically its mr. Wright lol. I love making jokes all the time. Hey, knock knock. Hey, you're supposed to say who's there! Lol I'm just kidding. Most women want a man with a sense of humor and that's me. Lol!!!

Less

Sent 6:26 PM

Start Message...   Send

Massage Date

A massage can be a relaxing way
to get to know someone.

Massage Date

1:53 AM 100%

< **Compose** Edit

30, Redlands, California

February 2

Hey I was gonna get a massage but then I saw your profile. So how about you come over and if you rub my back, I'll pay for dinner. I have all the proper oils and a youtube tutorial. Nothing sexual. It's gonna be on the living room couch with my swim trunks on and my roommates will be around. If this sounds weird, trust me, it's not. I always do this.

Less

Start Message... Send

Live Studio Audience

Create a memorable date by being in a live taping for TV. These tickets are usually free and it will be an original date idea.

Live Studio Audience

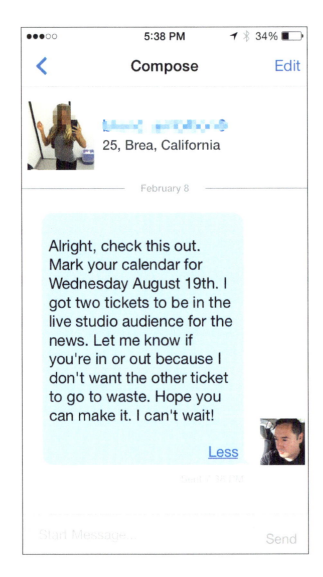

Relationship Ready

Most men are afraid of commitment. If you're ready for a serious relationship, let her know.

Relationship Ready

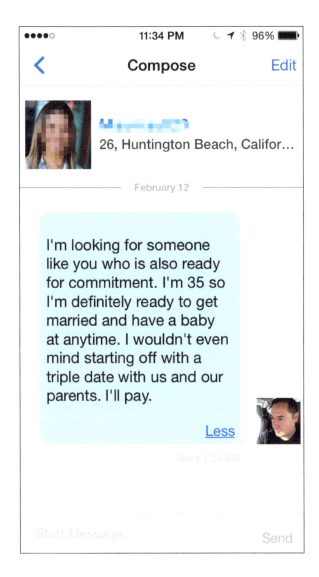

Class Reunion

If you have a high school reunion coming up, everybody will think you're doing ok if you show up with a hot date.

Class Reunion

11:01 AM · 43%

Compose　Edit

21, Moreno Valley, California

February 16

Hey you gotta help me out. I have a high school reunion coming up and I've been lying to everyone for years that I'm doing well. So I need to rent a porche and a tux and I need a hot date. If I show up without these things, Ron Brown will make fun of me. Help!

Less

Start Message...　Send

Pet Peeve
Talk about things you really dislike
before you agree to a date.

Pet Peeve

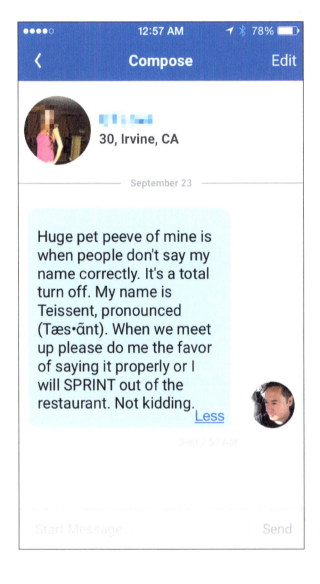

Good Guy

Let her know that even though you're not perfect, you're still a good person.

Good Guy

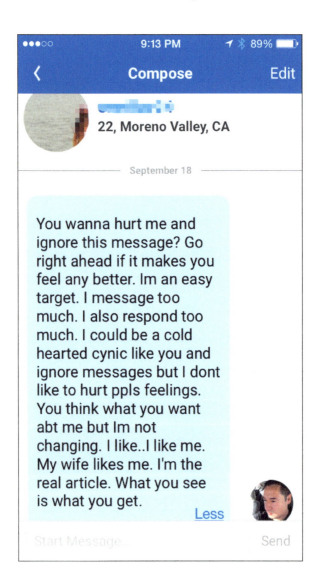

9:13 PM ✈ ✳ 89% ▭

‹ **Compose** Edit

22, Moreno Valley, CA

September 18

You wanna hurt me and ignore this message? Go right ahead if it makes you feel any better. Im an easy target. I message too much. I also respond too much. I could be a cold hearted cynic like you and ignore messages but I dont like to hurt ppls feelings. You think what you want abt me but Im not changing. I like..I like me. My wife likes me. I'm the real article. What you see is what you get.

Less

Start Message... Send

2nd Chance

When someone makes a mistake, it's not always over. Don't be above asking for a 2nd chance to salvage a relationship.

2nd Chance

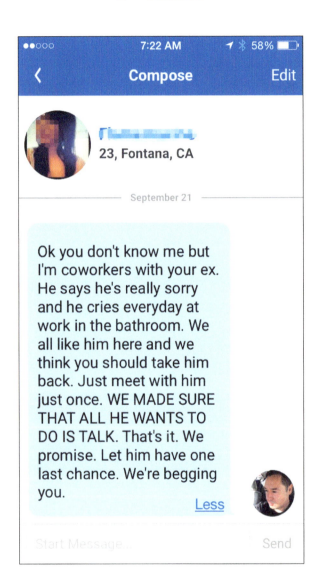

Which One?

Often girls will pose with their friends in pics. Make sure you're talking to the one you like.

Which One?

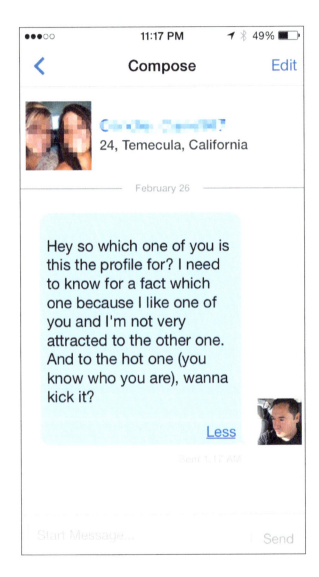

Be Who She Needs You To Be

Ask her what she's looking for in a man and see if you can fill those shoes.

Be Who She Needs You To Be

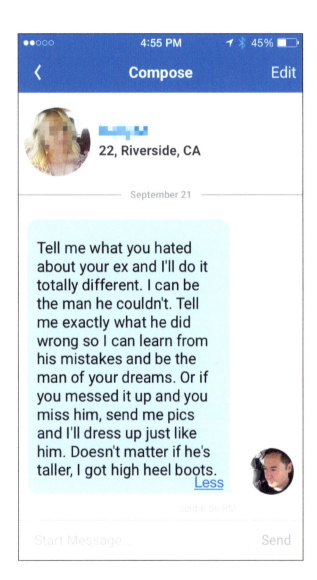

Tell me what you hated about your ex and I'll do it totally different. I can be the man he couldn't. Tell me exactly what he did wrong so I can learn from his mistakes and be the man of your dreams. Or if you messed it up and you miss him, send me pics and I'll dress up just like him. Doesn't matter if he's taller, I got high heel boots.

Less

Salesman Approach

Remember, you're selling yourself to this person. Use negotiating techniques as a salesman would.

Salesman Approach

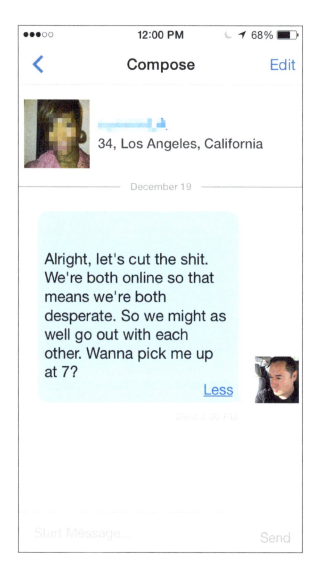

The Retort

When using the salesman approach,
if she fires back with a "no",
respond with an infallible point.

The Retort

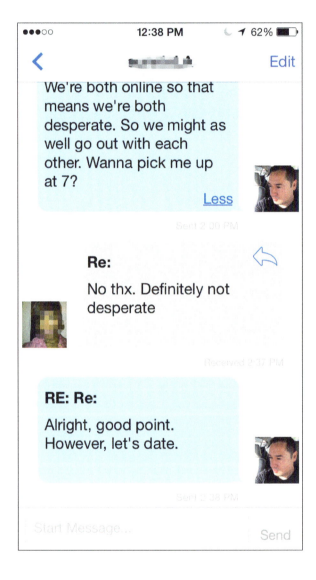

We're both online so that means we're both desperate. So we might as well go out with each other. Wanna pick me up at 7?

Less

Re:

No thx. Definitely not desperate

RE: Re:

Alright, good point. However, let's date.

Get Her Back

If a girl is cool enough to take care of you and take you out, remember that she did this and take care of her later.

Get Her Back

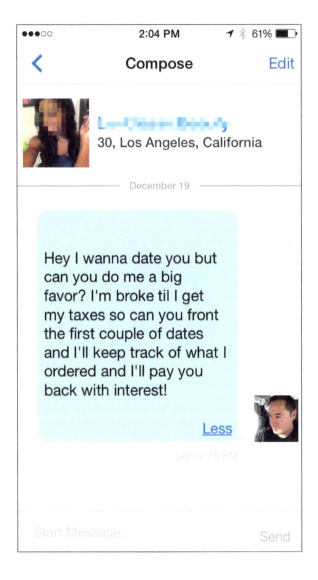

Raising Children
If there are kids in the mix,
talk about your views on parenting.

Raising Children

●●●○○   6:00 PM   ⚹ 93% ▰▱

< **Compose**   Edit

23, North Hollywood, California

December 21

So I see you have kids. I'm
a big believer in discipline
and punishment. A strict
home is the foundation of
good. Every president
we've ever had used to get
spanked. Google it.

Less

Start Message...   Send

Little Cockblockers

Kids get in the way of sex. Try to set up dates when the kids won't be a distraction.

Little Cockblockers

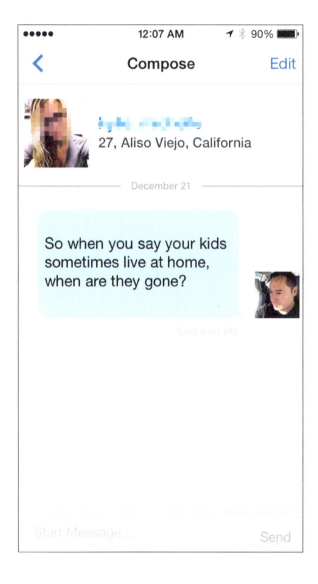

Christmas Opener

You can only use this opener once a year but talking about the holidays is a great way to feign actual interest.

Christmas Opener

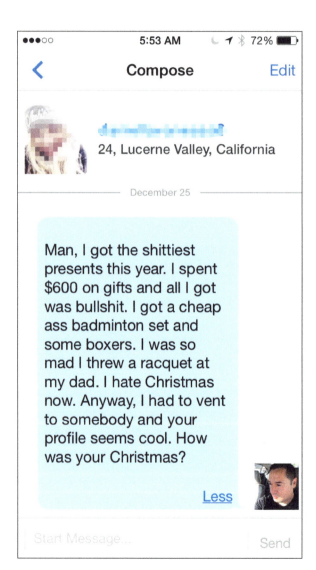

5:53 AM　72%

Compose　Edit

24, Lucerne Valley, California

December 25

Man, I got the shittiest presents this year. I spent $600 on gifts and all I got was bullshit. I got a cheap ass badminton set and some boxers. I was so mad I threw a racquet at my dad. I hate Christmas now. Anyway, I had to vent to somebody and your profile seems cool. How was your Christmas?

Less

Start Message...　Send

Flatter with Jealousy

Jealousy gets a bad rap. Girls actually like it and it makes them feel wanted. Show a little jealousy before you even meet.

Flatter with Jealousy

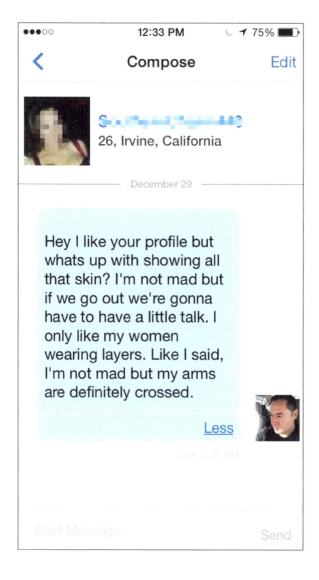

Not Lazy

A lot of girls like to hike, yoga, rock climb, etc. If you're job is physically demanding and leaves you with little energy, let her know that you want to date her without doing cardio.

Not Lazy

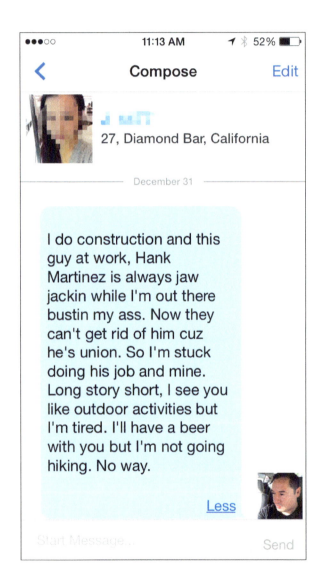

Look Out For Each Other

If you have a few friends that are also on the same site, you can let each other know about girls that are each others taste.

Look Out For Each Other

Something Different

A lot of times girls will try to flex their education with their vocabulary. Don't try to keep up. She's been around educated dudes already so show her something different.

Something Different

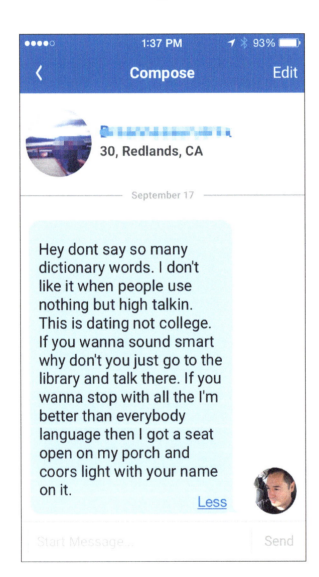

30, Redlands, CA

September 17

Hey dont say so many dictionary words. I don't like it when people use nothing but high talkin. This is dating not college. If you wanna sound smart why don't you just go to the library and talk there. If you wanna stop with all the I'm better than everybody language then I got a seat open on my porch and coors light with your name on it.

Less

Check Your Suspicions

Does something look off? Make her prove that your worries are false before you spend one dollar on her.

Check Your Suspicions

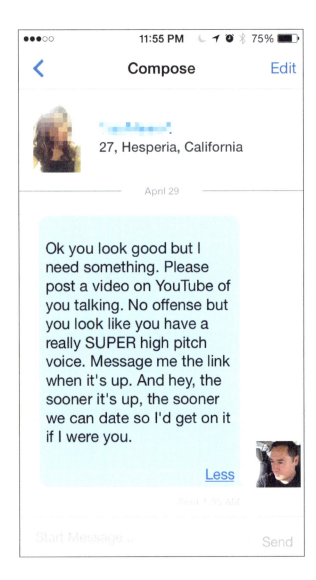

Honest Women

Finding an honest girl is tough so if you have the resources, take matters into your own hands to check things out.

Honest Women

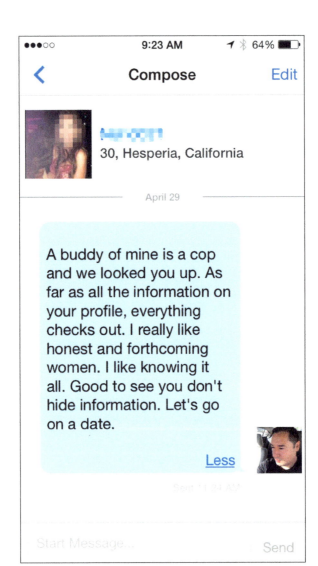

Guarding Wealth

If you talk about how you're worried about girls going after you just for your stuff, it's a great way to subtly put out there that you're rich.

Guarding Wealth

Lie About Money

Lying about money is the oldest trick in the book. Here's a slick one you can use.

Lie About Money

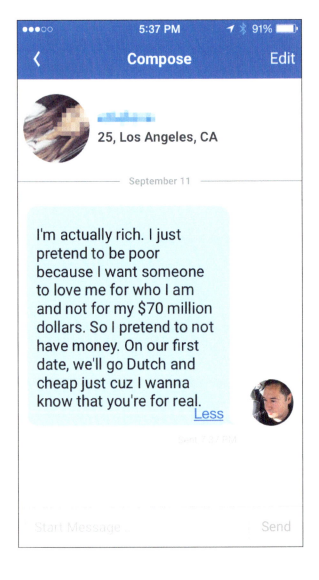

I'm actually rich. I just pretend to be poor because I want someone to love me for who I am and not for my $70 million dollars. So I pretend to not have money. On our first date, we'll go Dutch and cheap just cuz I wanna know that you're for real.

Be Friendly

If you want a relationship with a girl that's a mom, show that you'd like to be cool with the father of her children.

Be Friendly

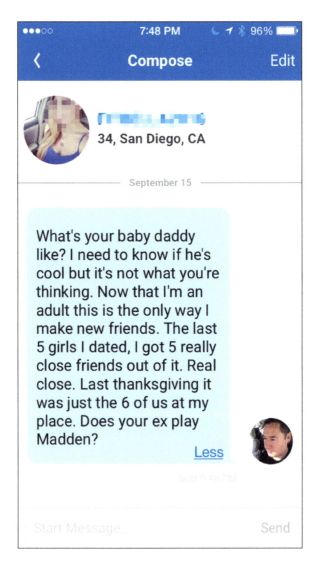

Safety 2nd

Hard for her to say no when you're willing to sacrifice your health and safety just to be around her.

Safety 2nd

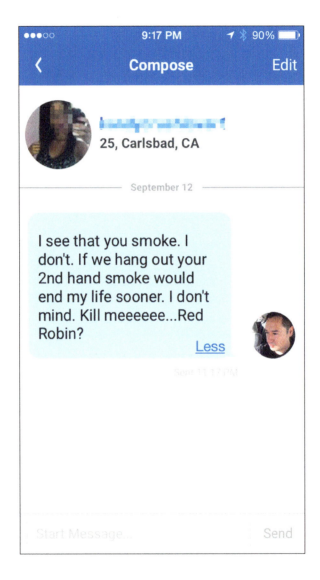

Friends With Benefits
Making friends on dating sites can lead to some serious perks.

Friends With Benefits

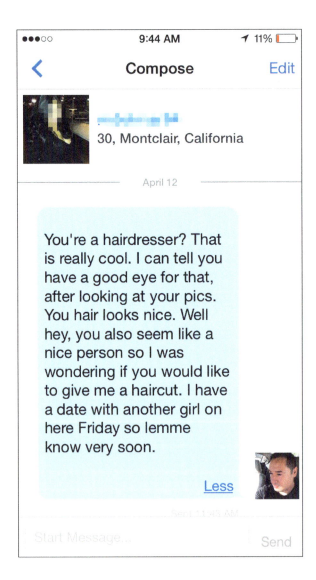

9:44 AM ✦ 11% ▭

< **Compose** **Edit**

30, Montclair, California

April 12

You're a hairdresser? That is really cool. I can tell you have a good eye for that, after looking at your pics. You hair looks nice. Well hey, you also seem like a nice person so I was wondering if you would like to give me a haircut. I have a date with another girl on here Friday so lemme know very soon.

Less

Start Message...   Send

Hard To Get

If you're a nobody, raise your social value by playing hard to get.

Hard To Get

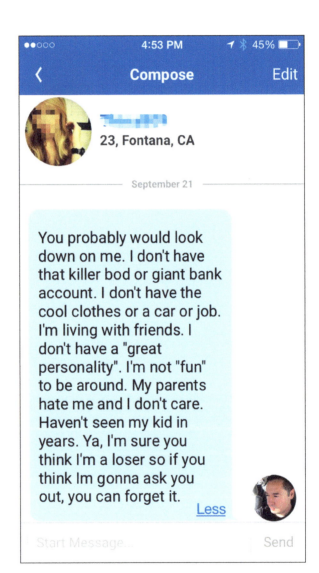

Number Close

Once you get the girls number, you're home free. Think of creative ways of getting it so you don't come off weird.

Number Close

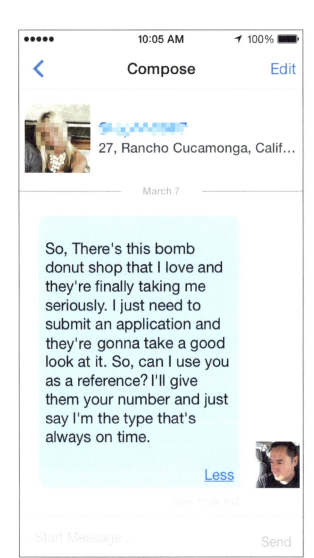

Be Exciting

Pretend to be someone that's more exciting than your boring ass self. A go-to move of mine is to ask her to help solve a crime. It'll make you look rad.

Be Exciting

Get Closure

There's this new fad going on of women just not responding when they lose interest. It's gonna happen but do your best to try to get a response so you know where you're at.

Get Closure

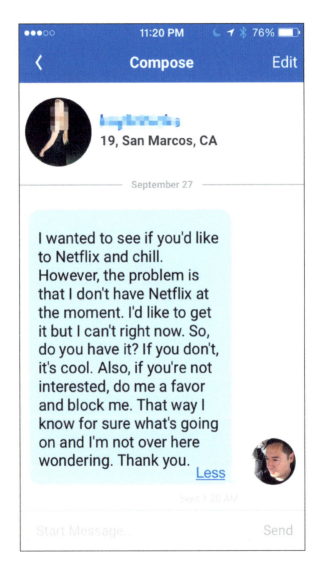

Cliffhanger

Provoke a response by using a cliffhanger in your message.

Cliffhanger

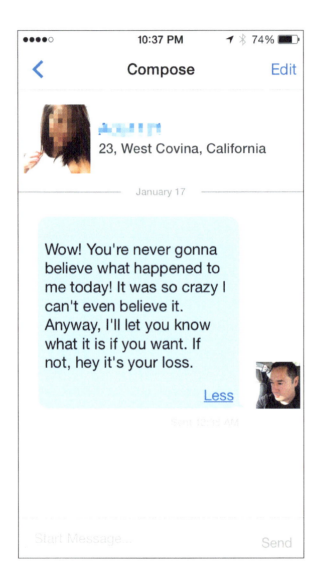

Smart With Money

Send her a message inviting her out but also showing her that you know how to save cash. Chicks love that.

Smart With Money

●●●○○   1:08 PM   ⌁ ⚹ 77% ▰▭

❮   **Compose**   Edit

28, Yorba Linda, California

January 17

Saturday mornings I like to go yard sale shopping in nice neighborhoods. Lots of good stuff can be found. Last week I spent $14 and I got a nice pleather jacket and a saw. They have stuff for girls too. They had a nice make up kit and all kinds of lip sticks. Come out with me and I'll show you the good spots.

Less

Start Message...   Send

Help People
Its not always about you. Once in a while use your account to help out the less fortunate.

Help People

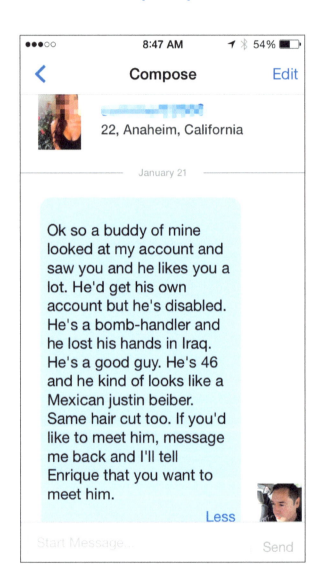

●●●○○   8:47 AM   ✈ ⁂ 54% ▬▮

<   **Compose**   Edit

22, Anaheim, California

January 21

Ok so a buddy of mine looked at my account and saw you and he likes you a lot. He'd get his own account but he's disabled. He's a bomb-handler and he lost his hands in Iraq. He's a good guy. He's 46 and he kind of looks like a Mexican justin beiber. Same hair cut too. If you'd like to meet him, message me back and I'll tell Enrique that you want to meet him.

Less

Start Message...   Send

Multitask

Show that you're a man that can get things done.
She'll respect that.

Multitask

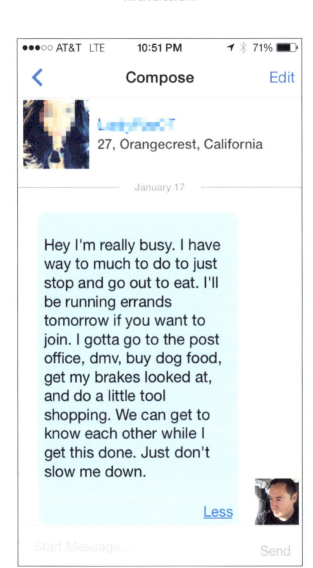

●●●○○ AT&T LTE   10:51 PM   ⌅ ⁂ 71% ▬

⟨   **Compose**   Edit

27, Orangecrest, California

———— January 17 ————

Hey I'm really busy. I have way to much to do to just stop and go out to eat. I'll be running errands tomorrow if you want to join. I gotta go to the post office, dmv, buy dog food, get my brakes looked at, and do a little tool shopping. We can get to know each other while I get this done. Just don't slow me down.

Less

Start Message...   Send

Ride Or Die Chick

If you're looking for a girl that's going to stick by your side, be open about whatever hardship you're going through.

Ride Or Die Chick

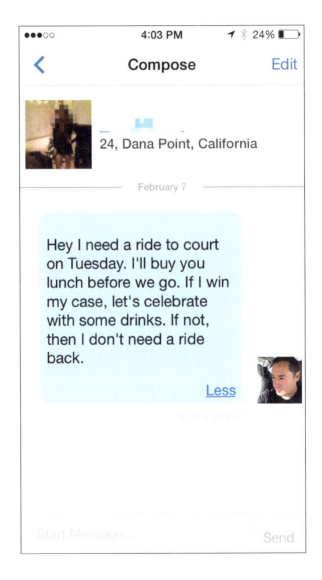

Be Tempting

Create a tempting situation and describe it. Paint a picture that will make her jump in her car and run red lights to get to you.

Be Tempting

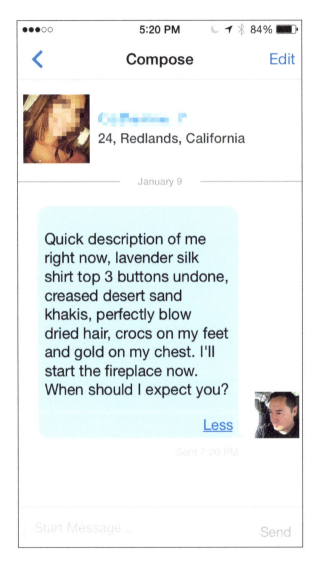

Exotic Pet

If you have an exotic pet, talk about it and get her to come over and check it out.

Exotic Pet

11:47 AM 38%

< **Compose** Edit

24, Riverside, California

February 24

I have a Macaw named "Bro". He's my best friend and I've trained him to be my "wing man" lol. We look at profiles together and he said "girlfriend" at your pic. Also, if we start doing stuff in front of him, he'll ask if I need a condom and then say "have fun". How cool, right?? Let's, the 3 of us, have dinner soon.

Less

Start Message... Send

Be Independent

Show that you *want* to hang out with her but you don't *need* to hang out with her.

Be Independent

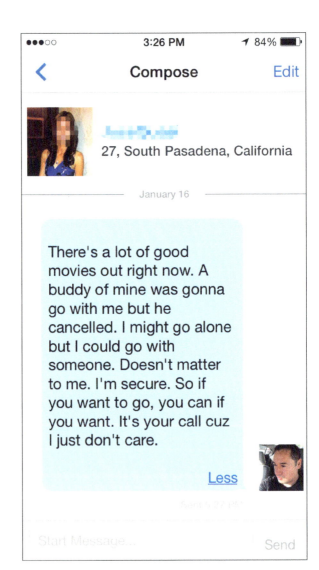

There's a lot of good movies out right now. A buddy of mine was gonna go with me but he cancelled. I might go alone but I could go with someone. Doesn't matter to me. I'm secure. So if you want to go, you can if you want. It's your call cuz I just don't care.

Not Just Sex

Sex isn't everything. Talk about other things you have going for you if you happen to be sexually disabled.

Not Just Sex

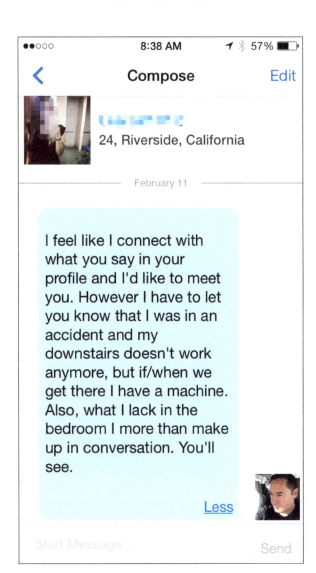

Wisdom Over Knowledge

Women look for men that are educated but if you're not, life experience can be used as a better substitute.

Wisdom Over Knowledge

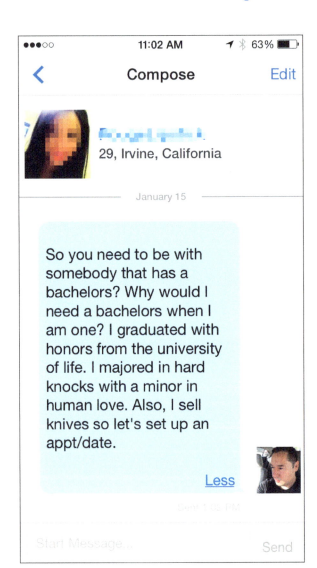

So you need to be with somebody that has a bachelors? Why would I need a bachelors when I am one? I graduated with honors from the university of life. I majored in hard knocks with a minor in human love. Also, I sell knives so let's set up an appt/date.

Less

Be Ambitious

Show that you're ambitious about work.

Be Ambitious

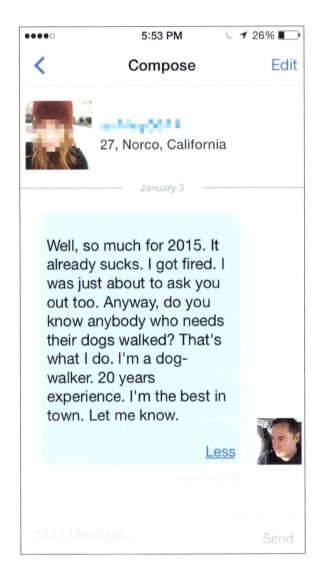

Good Job Chicks

Try to find a girl with a good job. Compliment her career choice. This will make her feel at ease with you and hopefully guilt her into paying for you.

Good Job Chicks

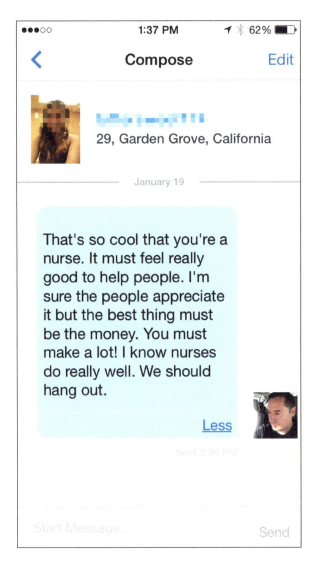

Mutual Acquaintance

If you recognize someone and you both know somebody, talk to her about what's going on with that person.

Mutual Acquaintance

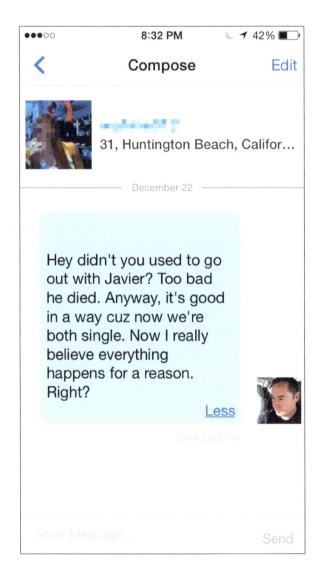

Older and Better

Ok, maybe you're a little older than what she likes but who cares? Tell her what you can do for her as an older man with life experience.

Older and Better

●●●○○   7:56 AM   ⌁ ⚡ 74% ▬▮

‹   **Compose**   **Edit**

21, Redlands, California

January 8

I see I'm way older than what you're looking for but I can fix things around the house. I'm handy. I know tile, masonry, block work, dry wall, roofing, electrical and everything. I just fixed a door yesterday. To show you how good you'd have it, if we go out to dinner just once, I'll make you a chair.

Less

Start Message   Send

Dating Tip

It doesn't matter what anybody else does for you, choose to take care of your date instead of other people.

Dating Tip

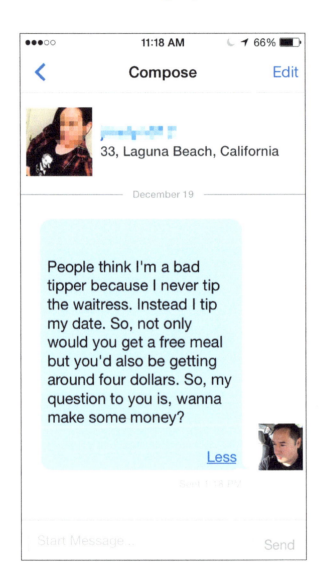

People think I'm a bad tipper because I never tip the waitress. Instead I tip my date. So, not only would you get a free meal but you'd also be getting around four dollars. So, my question to you is, wanna make some money?

Too Good To Be True

If you make a very nice offer and she doesn't believe you, reassure her that you're for real.

Too Good To Be True

Unbelievable

Keep reassuring her if she doesn't believe the great opportunity that you're offering.

Unbelievable

taxed on a percentage of their sales. I could write you a book to why I would never date you, just for not tipping your server and why it's better for everyone if you did. I almost don't believe you, its that ridiculous--giving money to your date!? Lol

Less

RE:

Tell me how ridiculous it is at the end of the year when you have over $180. Trust me, you'll love it

Warn Her

If you start to lose interest, let her know that she's in jeopardy of ruining the connection.

Warn Her

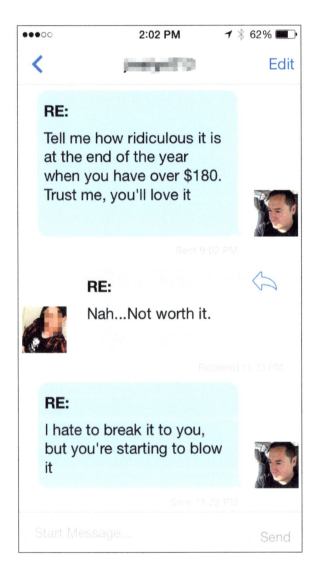

Double Date

Inviting her to a double date could raise your chances. Also there's less pressure for you to act cool the whole time.

Double Date

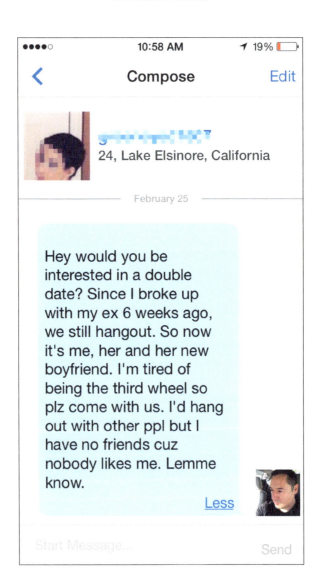

Disneydick

Disneyland is almost a guarantee! If you can afford it, Donald Duck is an amazing wing man.

Disneydick

1:16 PM · ◯ ◀ ✳ 21% ▮

‹   **Compose**   Edit

24, San Bernardino, California

February 17

Hey come to Disneyland with me. I'm sooo tired of going alone. I still love it but I'm tired of riding the teacups by myself. I was thinking if we hit it off, we can get on splash mountain and get a little closer. If not, we can just be friends and get on the haunted mansion. You down?

Less

Start Message...   Send

Passive Passive

Some girls are very controlling. Hey, let 'em.

Passive Passive

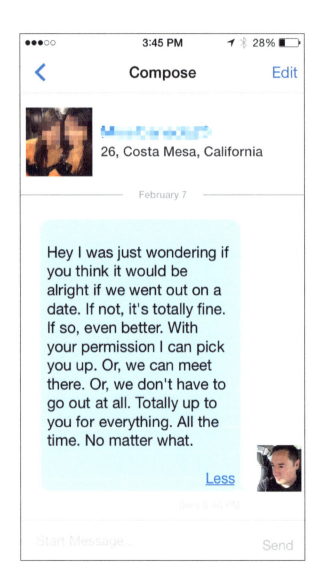

Still Around

If you have a connection with your ex, explain why.

Still Around

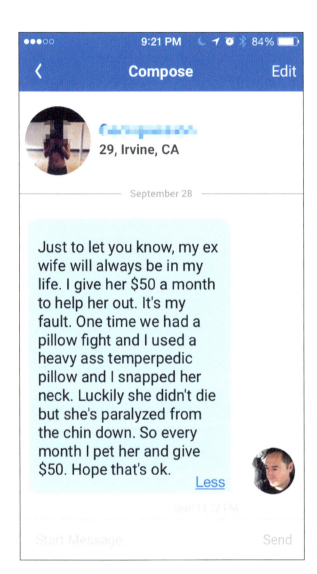

9:21 PM　　84%

‹　　**Compose**　　**Edit**

29, Irvine, CA

September 28

Just to let you know, my ex wife will always be in my life. I give her $50 a month to help her out. It's my fault. One time we had a pillow fight and I used a heavy ass temperpedic pillow and I snapped her neck. Luckily she didn't die but she's paralyzed from the chin down. So every month I pet her and give $50. Hope that's ok.

Less

Start Message...　　Send

Ride-along

If you have an adventurous job, show her some excitement and bring her with you to work one day.

Ride-along

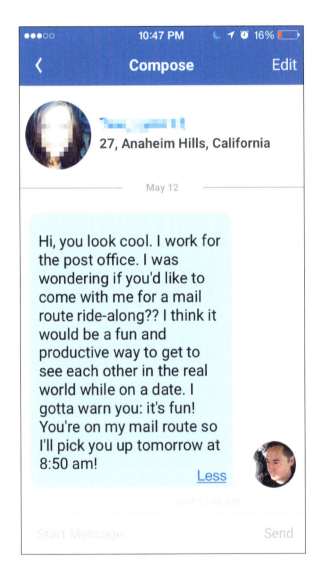

10:47 PM · 16%

Compose Edit

27, Anaheim Hills, California

May 12

Hi, you look cool. I work for the post office. I was wondering if you'd like to come with me for a mail route ride-along?? I think it would be a fun and productive way to get to see each other in the real world while on a date. I gotta warn you: it's fun! You're on my mail route so I'll pick you up tomorrow at 8:50 am!

Less

Start Message Send

Describe Limitations

If you can't go certain places, let her know so you can plan a better date.

Describe Limitations

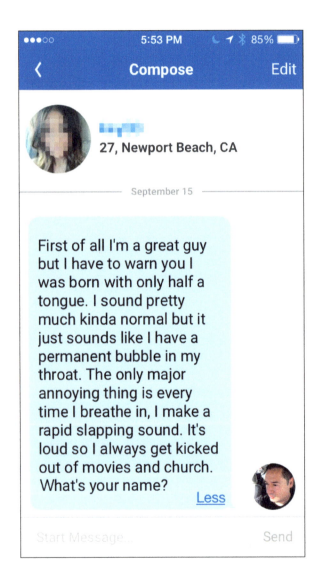

Get A Replacement
Don't be brokenhearted over an ex.
Just get another one.

Get A Replacement

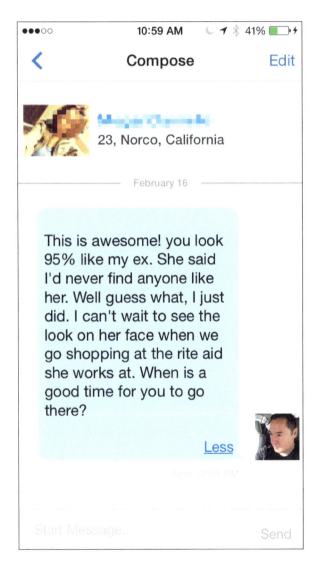

This is awesome! you look 95% like my ex. She said I'd never find anyone like her. Well guess what, I just did. I can't wait to see the look on her face when we go shopping at the rite aid she works at. When is a good time for you to go there?

They're Scared Of You

Remember, women see men as bigger animal that can kill them. Don't scare her away. Try to think of her as a scared deer and talk to her like that.

They're Scared Of You

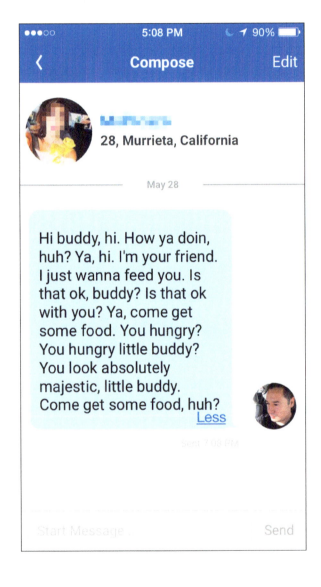

Use Uber

Use uber for your date if you can.

Use Uber

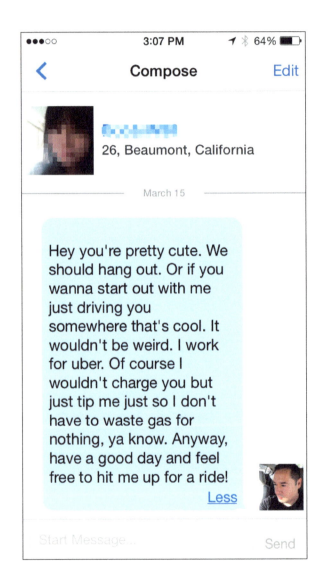

Be High Class
Show off your classy ass self.

Be High Class

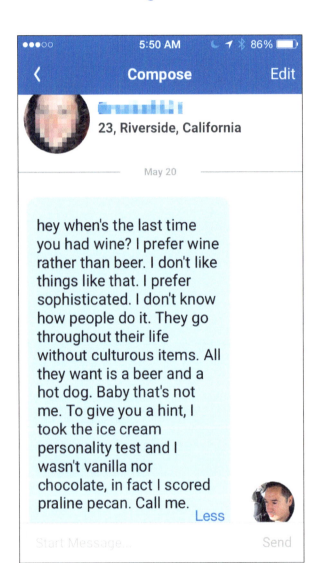

Be Strong
Chicks love it when you're buff.

Be Strong

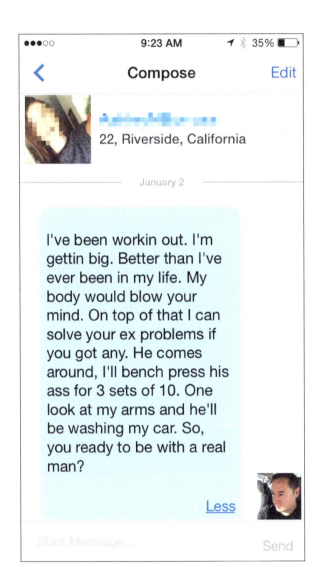

Make Her Less

Ok, let's say she's looking for a guy that's way better than you. That's fine. Just cut her down.

Make Her Less

Family Fortune

If you came up on some money from your
family, definitely let her know.
Money is always great.

Family Fortune

Parade Date

Parades are free. Take advantage of a
free date whenever you can.

Parade Date

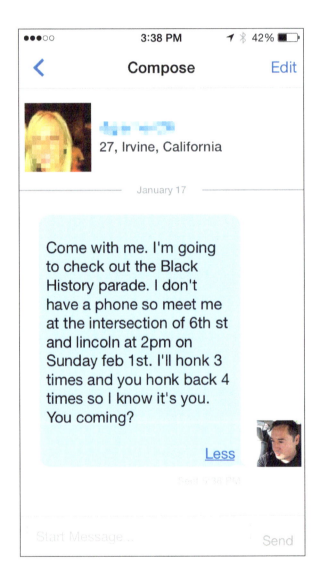

Be Kind To All
Kindness and gentleness
will make the ladies smile.

Be Kind To All

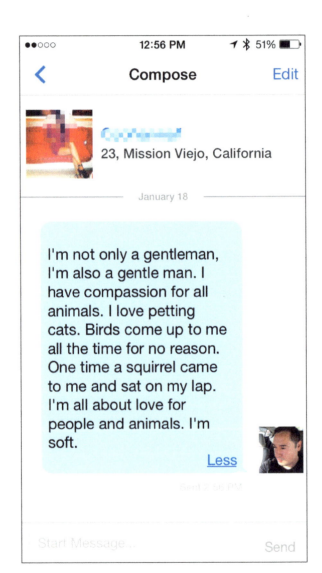

Make Her Feel Racist

This is one of the very best ways to guilt a woman into a date.

Make Her Feel Racist

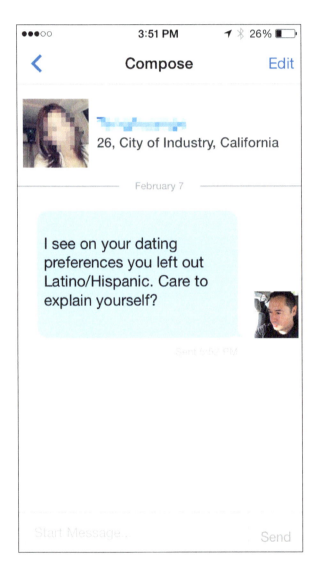

Celebrate With Her
If you have something to celebrate, invite her.
Everybody wants to party with a winner.

Celebrate With Her

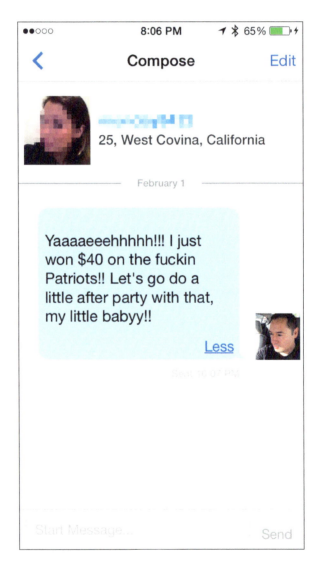

No Money, Don't Ask

If you're broke like most of us are, then don't ask her out. Make her ask you out so when the bill comes out, you can use the old chick phrase "Well, since you asked me out, you have to pay." Have fun and eat up!

No Money, Don't Ask

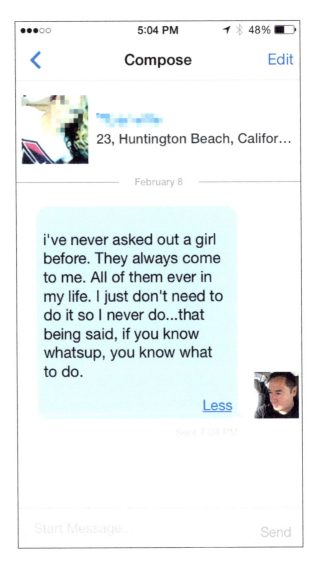

Sympathy Play

If you ever get stood up, message a chick and tell her about it. She'll probably feel bad for you and want to hook up.

Sympathy Play

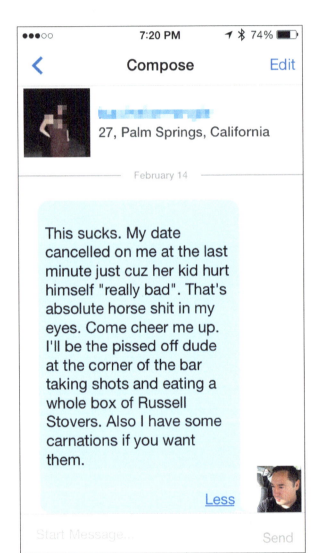

Go Camping

Camping is a totally cheap date. If you see she likes camping on her profile, invite her to a cheap camping date.

Go Camping

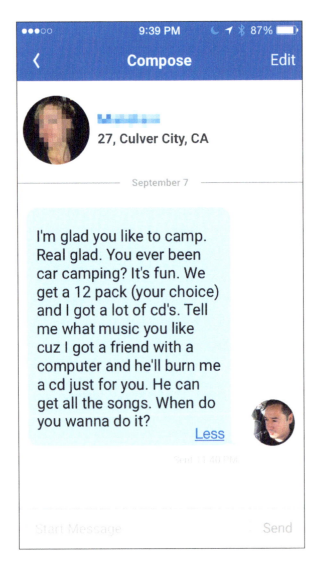

Real Her

Chicks always have pics of them at their best. Get a better idea of what you're going to see by asking her to put a picture of a real life situation that you're used to seeing.

Real Her

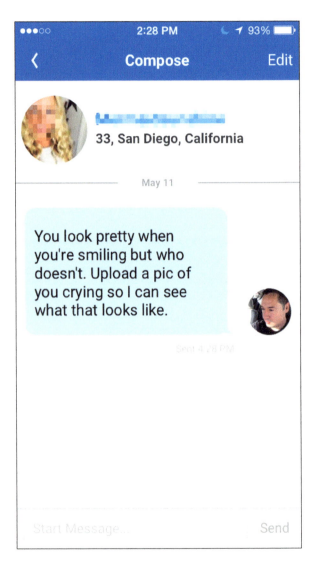

Call Her Out

In most dating sites you can see who's viewed you. If they click on your profile and don't say anything, don't let that rudeness slide.

Call Her Out

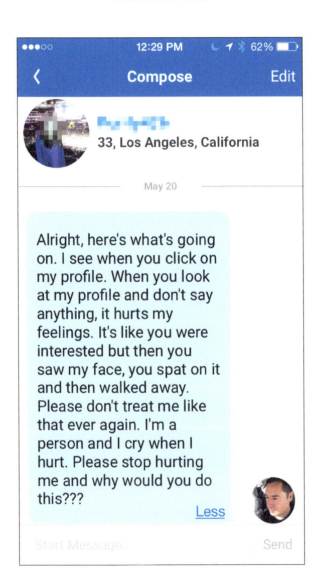

Alright, here's what's going on. I see when you click on my profile. When you look at my profile and don't say anything, it hurts my feelings. It's like you were interested but then you saw my face, you spat on it and then walked away. Please don't treat me like that ever again. I'm a person and I cry when I hurt. Please stop hurting me and why would you do this???

Stand Out

There's a lot of guys messaging her every day. Acknowledge this and let her know how much you want to date her.

Stand Out

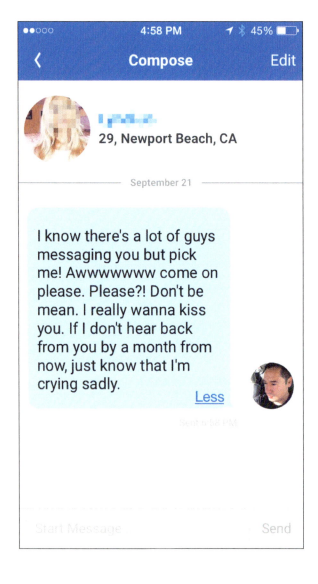

I know there's a lot of guys messaging you but pick me! Awwwwwww come on please. Please?! Don't be mean. I really wanna kiss you. If I don't hear back from you by a month from now, just know that I'm crying sadly.

Less

Show Your Stuff

If you have a lot of collectors items,
show it off to girls. It'll get them excited.

Show Your Stuff

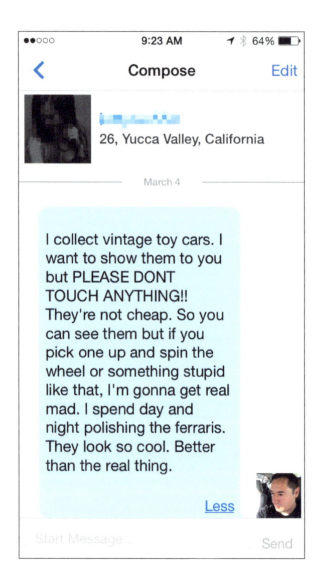

Play Date

The quickest way to a mom is to set up a play date.

Play Date

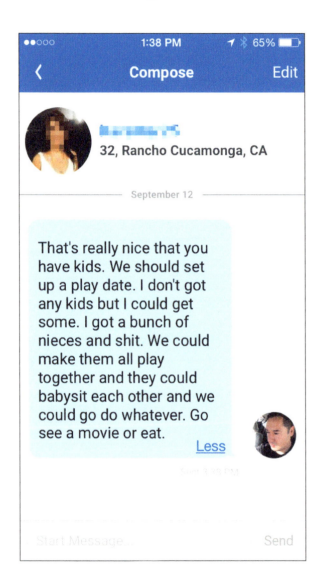

Welcome Her Back
If you see someone is back online, say hello.

Welcome Her Back

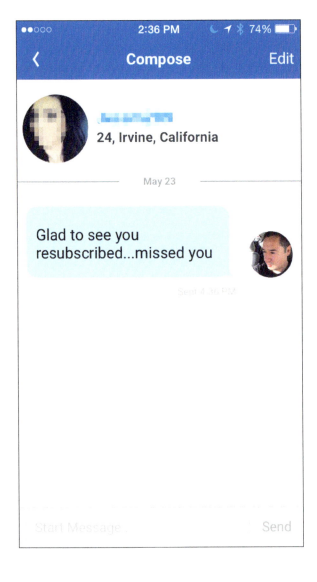

Cougars

If you're looking for just a hook up, cougars usually want the same thing. And hey, the older the better!

Cougars

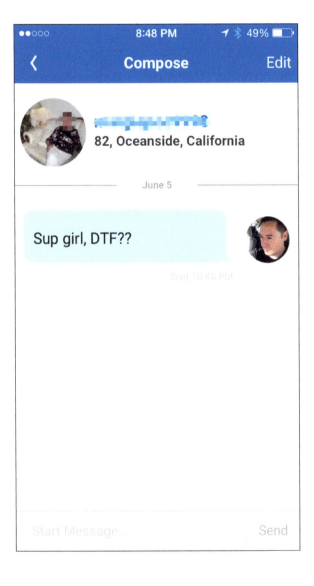

Tell Her A Secret

Form a connection by telling her a secret
that you don't tell many people.

Tell Her A Secret

Success Story

Share your success story and impress her.

Success Story

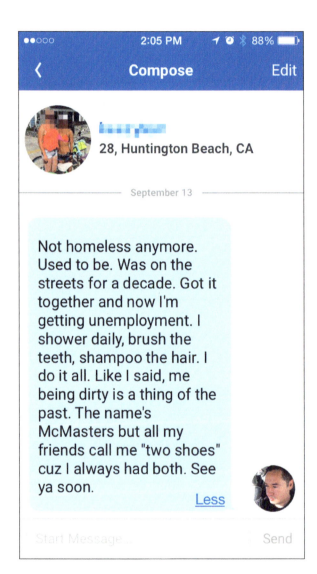

Compose Edit

2:05 PM ●●○○○ 88%

28, Huntington Beach, CA

September 13

Not homeless anymore. Used to be. Was on the streets for a decade. Got it together and now I'm getting unemployment. I shower daily, brush the teeth, shampoo the hair. I do it all. Like I said, me being dirty is a thing of the past. The name's McMasters but all my friends call me "two shoes" cuz I always had both. See ya soon.

Less

Start Message... Send

Feel Her Out

If you're into some freaky stuff In the bedroom, mention some things you're into.

Feel Her Out

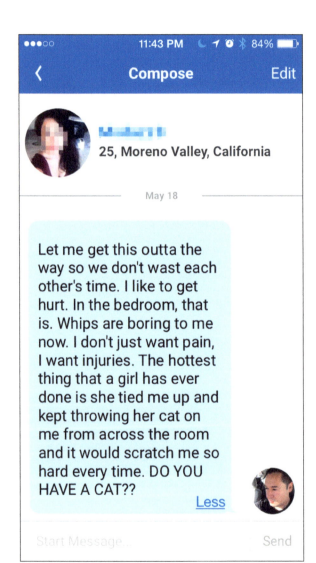

Be Decisive

Girls want guys who know how to make decisions. Be a man and call the shots when you go on dates. Try to think like an umpire.

Be Decisive

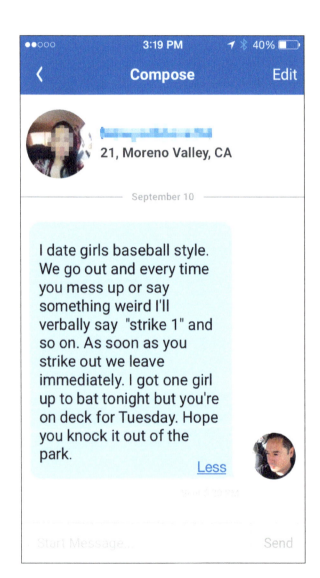

Keep It Flowing
Conversation is an art.
Try to have smooth segues.

Keep It Flowing

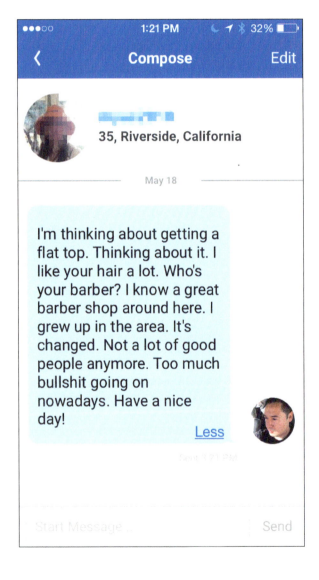

Explain Why You're Single
Girls want to know why so just tell them.

Explain Why You're Single

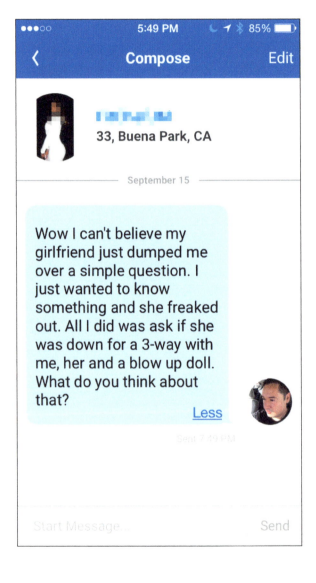

Offer What You Can

You might not have a lot going for you but tell her what you do have to offer.

Offer What You Can

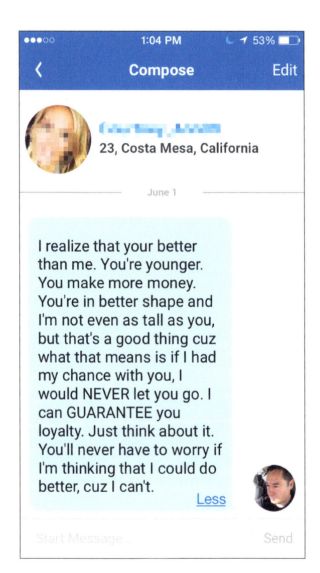

When You Get A Like

If a girl likes one of your pics, bring it up.
There was definitely something there.

When You Get A Like

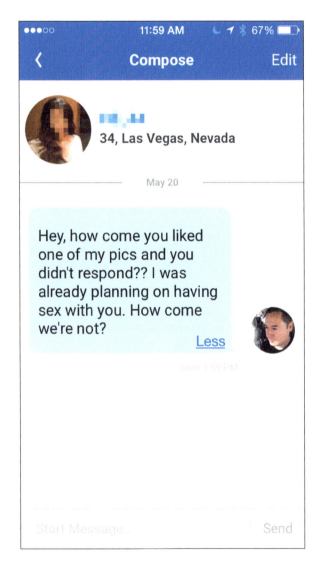

Cook

Cook food and that'll get them right over.

Cook

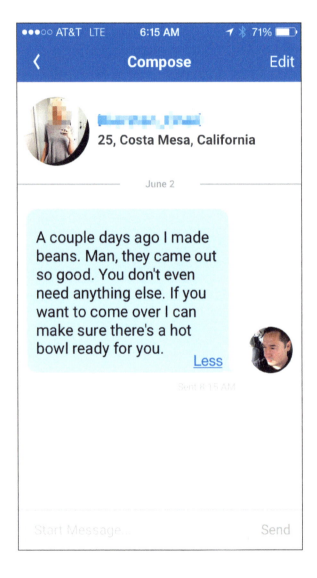

●●●○○ AT&T LTE   6:15 AM   ⏶ ✶ 71% ▬▭

❮   **Compose**   Edit

25, Costa Mesa, California

June 2

A couple days ago I made beans. Man, they came out so good. You don't even need anything else. If you want to come over I can make sure there's a hot bowl ready for you.   Less

Sent 8:15 AM

Start Message...   Send

Wear A Suit
Chicks go absolutely insane over suits.

Wear A Suit

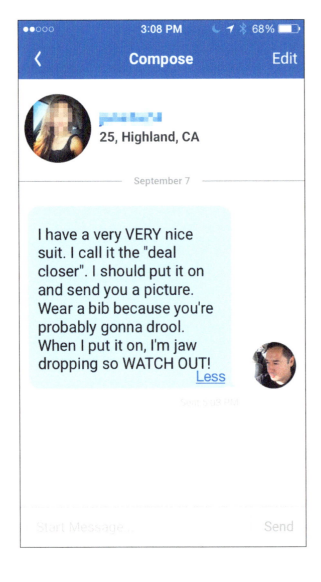

Positive Energy
A positive attitude is very attractive.
Try to be as positive as you can.

Positive Energy

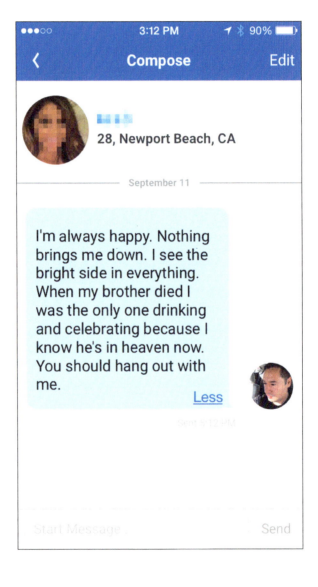

Exercise Date
If you see someone is athletic,
invite them to a work out.

Exercise Date

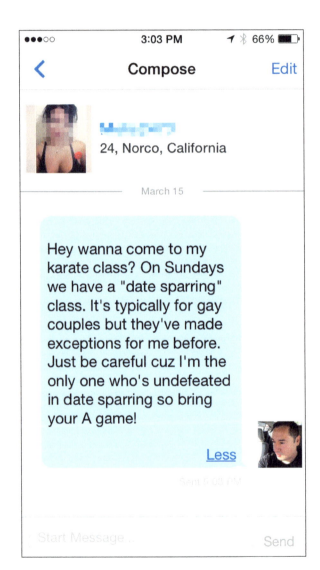

Compose

24, Norco, California

March 15

Hey wanna come to my karate class? On Sundays we have a "date sparring" class. It's typically for gay couples but they've made exceptions for me before. Just be careful cuz I'm the only one who's undefeated in date sparring so bring your A game!

Less

Family Opener
Ask her about her family to start a genuine convo.

Family Opener

New Years Resolution
Send a message talking about your goals.

New Years Resolution

See It All

Ask her to upload more pics if you don't feel you have the whole picture of what she looks like.

See It All

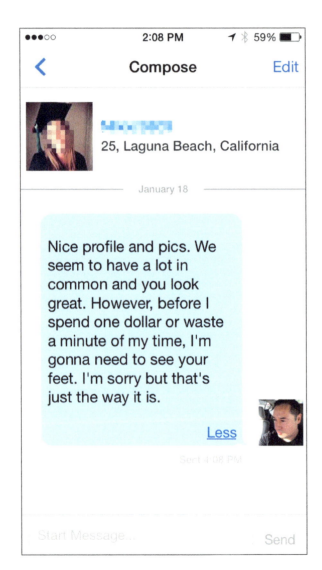

Find A Way

Nothing should stop you from approaching a girl for a date, not even a physical handicap.

Find A Way

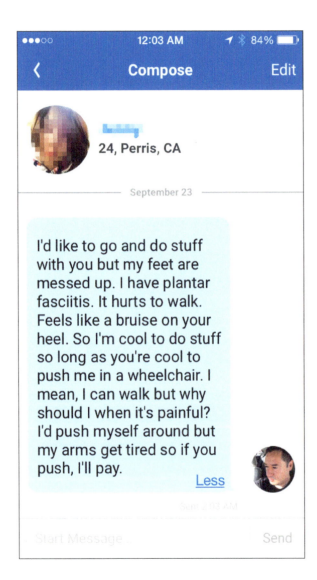

24, Perris, CA

September 23

I'd like to go and do stuff with you but my feet are messed up. I have plantar fasciitis. It hurts to walk. Feels like a bruise on your heel. So I'm cool to do stuff so long as you're cool to push me in a wheelchair. I mean, I can walk but why should I when it's painful? I'd push myself around but my arms get tired so if you push, I'll pay.

Less

Ready To Go
Let her know that you're ready to start dating.

Ready To Go

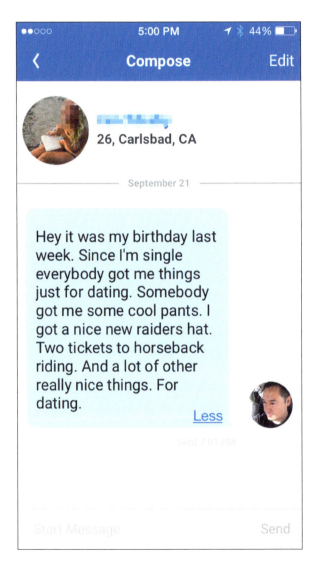

Weakness Into Strength

If there's something weird about you, try to flip it into originality instead of calling it weird.

Weakness Into Strength

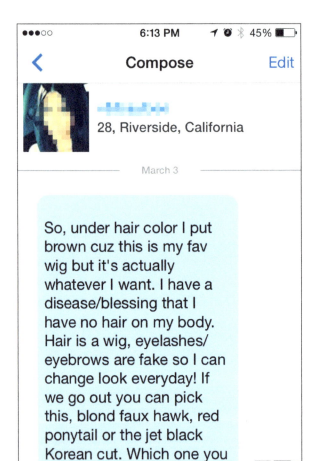

So, under hair color I put brown cuz this is my fav wig but it's actually whatever I want. I have a disease/blessing that I have no hair on my body. Hair is a wig, eyelashes/eyebrows are fake so I can change look everyday! If we go out you can pick this, blond faux hawk, red ponytail or the jet black Korean cut. Which one you want?

Middle Eastern Ladies

Middle Easterns are some of the most beautiful girls out there, but try to get a feel of the culture and customs before you approach them.

Middle Eastern Ladies

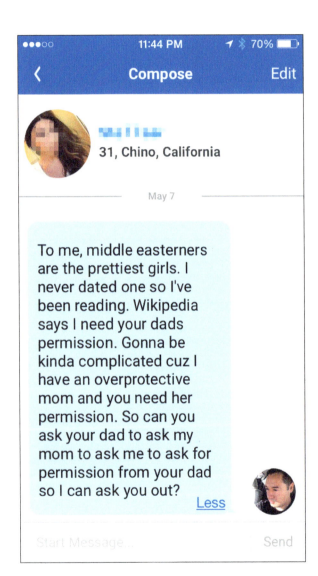

> 11:44 PM 70%
>
> **Compose** Edit
>
> 31, Chino, California
>
> May 7
>
> To me, middle easterners are the prettiest girls. I never dated one so I've been reading. Wikipedia says I need your dads permission. Gonna be kinda complicated cuz I have an overprotective mom and you need her permission. So can you ask your dad to ask my mom to ask me to ask for permission from your dad so I can ask you out?
>
> Less
>
> Start Message ... Send

New Account

Try all of these techniques and I'm sure you'll get laid. If not, its probably an account issue. You know how computers are so just open another one and reach out again.

New Account

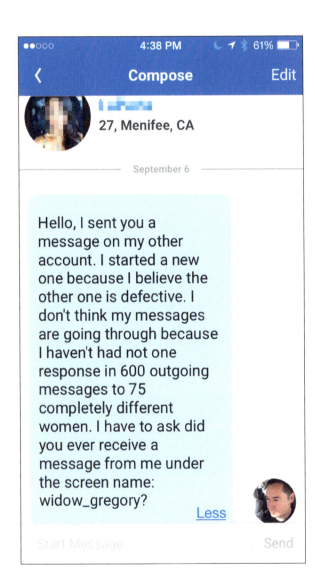

About The Author

Alfonso Ochoa is a stand up comedian with almost a decade of experience in comedy writing and even more experience at failing with women. This book showcases that he is talented at both.

Learn More

For more advice, follow me on Twitter and Instagram
@matchmastr

Also, feel free to tag the **@matchmastr** if you have some
knowledge and lessons that you would like to share.

CPSIA information can be obtained
at www.ICGtesting.com
Printed in the USA
FSOW03n1424040316
17514FS